TH

STRAITJACKET
OF
PERFECTIONISM

How to Stop Chasing 'Perfect' and Finally Achieve Your Greatest Goals

JOHN CONNOR

THE STRAITJACKET OF PERFECTIONISM

By John Connor

Interior Design: Christina Culbertson, 3CsBooks.com

ISBN-978-0-9985958-2-5

Shannon Publishing, LLC
PO Box 92468
Austin TX 78749-2468

ADVANCE PRAISE FOR *THE STRAITJACKET OF PERFECTIONISM*…

"I have lived a creative life as a singer songwriter for over fifty years. Yet, locked away inside my perfectionist heart is a restrained longing to paint and to write books. I give thanks to John Connor for his insightful and illuminating book The Straightjacket of Perfectionism — he has provided me a key to free my creative soul. I recommend this book to stymied perfectionists everywhere."

— Dana Cooper
Singer-Songwriter

"This is a little gem of a book that reveals the traps we have set for ourselves, shows us how to escape them, and frees us to run toward the things we have always wanted to do and be. John Connor offers insight into our under-achievement patterns that can completely upend them and gives us tools to use to get traction toward our dreams. Resist the urge to procrastinate and read this now!"

— Rev. Karen Tudor,
Unity of New Braunfels, TX
2017 Chair of the Board of Trustees
Unity Worldwide Ministries

"Well written and entertaining, this book is full of helpful advice. I recognized myself in some of the stories - and I bet you will too! Don't waste time criticizing yourself. Use your time instead reading this book and trying the tips within it!"

— Cindy Wigglesworth
Author of *SQ21: The Twenty-One Skills of Spiritual Intelligence*

TABLE OF CONTENTS

DEDICATION

To my parents, Jim and Cierra Connor — you lived wonderful lives of loving service, and were always a great support to me.

To Bonnie Connor — once my wife, and always the amazing mother of our children. You were there when I first gave the talk that this book is based on. Thank you for so many things, including our continued friendship.

INTRODUCTION

I had no idea I was a perfectionist. Perfectionists are the people you hear about who yell at other people a lot—movie directors, sports coaches, business managers—people that are never satisfied with anyone else's work.

Not me. I am pretty easygoing about what other people do.

I'm not the kind of person who has an immaculately clean and organized desk, office, or house. (I am writing these words at my dining table because my desk is covered with papers!) So how could I be a perfectionist?

I stumbled upon this by accident when taking the DISC assessment (Dominance, Influence, Support, and Caution), a personality profile tool used by companies for hiring and training. The test results produce one of 15 classic patterns and among them is Perfectionism.

While the generated results seemed mostly accurate, the high perfectionism score threw me because, as I said above, I didn't fit any of my assumptions about perfectionists. But my assumptions were based on my ideas about what are called, "other-oriented perfectionists." It turns out I am a "self-oriented perfectionist," and you may be too if you were drawn to this book. I don't yell at other people; I yell at myself in my head. I don't humiliate others with accusations of failure; I humiliate myself. The only person I hold to unreasonably high standards is *me*.

The kinder flavor of self-criticism tends to be "You're not good enough," and "You probably won't get this right," and "You are smart, but how can you be so stupid?" The more aggressive self-talk includes things like, "Don't be such a dumb-ass! Who the hell do you think you are even to *try* that?"

The good news? I've gotten a lot better using the strategies and new thinking that I describe in this book. In a nutshell, I tried new things, cut back on my internal berating criticism, and became more courageous and happy. My adventures have included stand-up comedy, making a short film and successfully submitting it to a film festival, finishing my college degree as an "Adult Learner," and opening up to my spiritual growth.

For example, I decided to make a short film. Instead of being overwhelmed by all that would entail and that I had shot nothing more complicated than home videos of vacations, I asked my friend Dominic Cancilla for help. (He had worked on local commercials and went on to become a Producer of such films as *Machete.*) Dominic said we needed to do a "film test" to see if we had the right film stock for where we would shoot. Instead of shooting footage of trees and birds with that can of 16mm film, I wrote a fake trailer for a spoof movie. I enlisted a couple of friends to act in it, we shot it in one afternoon, and it turned out good enough to be accepted into some short film festivals. You can see the silliness on YouTube if you search for "El Hibachi."

One lesson I've learned is to ask a friend for help. The myriad things you'll realize you don't know, things stopping you in your perfectionistic tracks, get lifted when you receive some knowledgeable help.

It would be bad enough if perfectionism kept you from trying only new hobbies, learning a new language, and joining your friends at karaoke. And it does do all that. But the real harm is that perfectionism prevents you from following your dreams, from attempting the deepest desires of your heart, because it carries such a great internal risk if you fail.

An example of this is if, say, you want to write a novel. You will likely stop writing it a third of the way through the first draft. One reason is that you know you'll be crushed if you send it around to the publishing houses and they all reject it. That's because you have an internal sense that a great novelist is not only what you want to be, but maybe *Who You Are.* So the book either stays in your drawer or you tweak it here and there every few months. If you keep the book in your desk, it always "has potential" and might someday be ready to be sent out and published.

But the book's never ready, is it? So your dreams, your deepest desires, remain on hold.

You and I know deep down that this is no way to live. And we don't have to live that way. You can overcome chasing perfection and constantly failing to catch it. You can be someone who strives for excellence *and* who accepts mistakes and setbacks along the way.

The biggest mistake of all is to stop attempting anything in order to avoid making mistakes. Every ice skater, for example, falls down many times in the beginning. It is a given: You can't escape falling while you learn to skate. Yet those falls aren't failure, they are learning. As perfectionists, we make unrealistic assumptions about what our own standards of performance should be. So if we choose to ice-skate, we expect to be able to do a triple toe loop our first time out.

Come with me, and we will wrestle this inner perfectionist to the ground together. And then you'll be amazed at all the creativity and bravery within you, just waiting to come out.

CHAPTER 1

WHAT IS PERFECTIONISM?

WHO IS A PERFECTIONIST?

Nobody's perfect ... but practice makes perfect.

We strive for perfect health. We may hear, or want to hear, ourselves called a perfect student, perfect boss, or perfect spouse. On television and in entertainment magazines, we see slim, firm bodies that we are told are perfect. Home and garden magazines tell you how to throw a perfect party, set a perfect table, and cook the perfect summer meal.

We believe we can do all these things and that we can learn to do them perfectly. We can have the perfect home office, the perfect job, perhaps even perfect children. We believe, in short, in the perfectibility of humanity. Through technology or sheer effort, we'll fulfill every ambition.

Or, at least, *some* of us believe this. Many prominent Western thinkers have been more cautious. British writer Ben Jonson reminds us that "*in short measures* life may perfect be," while Robert Browning tells us that "what's come to perfection perishes." In her book, *Bird by Bird* Anne Lamott wrote, "Perfectionism is the voice of the oppressor, the enemy of the people."

Whether you're on the side of the poets or the perfectionists, this book is for you. I'll explain the dangers of perfectionism—creative, spiritual, and otherwise—and outline the steps you can take to move beyond this spiritually-draining and creativity-cramping trait. But before I do, I have an assessment to help you identify if this is a problem for you.

Perfectionism Self-Test

Do any of these apply to you?

- When I face a deadline, I usually procrastinate.
- I frequently leave projects unfinished. I get about a third of the way done then lose interest.

- When I finish a project or performance, I'm usually discouraged and disappointed in myself because I didn't do better.
- I wish my spouse/children/friends would get their acts together.
- I experience stage fright when I have to speak to or perform in front of a large group of people.
- I turn to drugs, alcohol, sex, or food for comfort when I'm feeling down. (Brené Brown, in her book *Daring Greatly*, describes these as "numbing" behaviors.)
- I enjoy competitions only when I'm the winner.
- I never seem able to achieve my goals.

If you agree with one or more of these statements, you may be a perfectionist. The rest of this book goes into greater depth about these issues.

What Is Perfectionism?

Perfectionism is the desire to be flawless. It is also the effort expended in striving toward this unrealistic goal.[1] Perfectionists believe that, through the right combination of calculation and behavior, we can become an ideal person. We crave the approval of others—especially peers and authority figures—and experience low self-esteem when we fail to achieve in areas that are important to us (and sometimes in areas that aren't).[2] In short, perfectionists fear failure, and because of this, we also tend to fear risk.[3]

Let's break this down a bit further. The Canadian researchers Gordon Flett and Paul Hewitt, affiliated with York University and the University of British Columbia, respectively, are widely published on perfectionism issues. They identify several types of perfectionism.

The *normal perfectionist* is a high-achieving person; he sets high but reasonable goals for himself, which leads to higher self-esteem. While Flett and Hewitt consider this person to be a perfectionist, I see this person pursuing not perfectionism but excellence. I call this person a *high achiever.*

The *other-oriented perfectionist* sets exceedingly high standards for other people. Not surprisingly, other-oriented perfectionists have a hard time maintaining healthy relationships because they tend to criticize others more often than they praise them.

People who suffer from *socially prescribed perfectionism* believe they must live up to an unrealistic standard set by their culture or society[4].

The *self-oriented perfectionist* sets personal standards that may be impossible to reach. Most people of this type practice perfectionistic self-presentation. They seek to display perfect behavior, conceal any signs of imperfection, and avoid admitting verbally to any mistakes or lack of perfect performance. Does this play out in your own life? Does this kind of thinking affect your life at church or in your athletic group? In other arenas?

What Causes Perfectionism?

Psychologists have identified factors that may contribute to perfectionism. Many are external ones that perfectionists internalize as unrealistic goals and irrational beliefs. These beliefs and goals—which often are so high as to be unattainable—create a cycle of trying and failing that is highlighted in Figure 1 (see page 17).

Parenting

For many perfectionists, much of the pressure to achieve at unrealistically high levels originates in their childhood and adolescence. Flett and Hewitt argue that perfectionist parents tend to instill perfectionistic beliefs and behaviors in their children. They identify four primary models through which this trait is passed.

Under the *social expectations model,* children learn that their parents will approve of them if they are perfect. These children may learn or believe that their parents' love is contingent upon their own continuing high achievement. Parents aren't the only source of social expectations. Teachers, coaches, clergy, and other authority figures may also lead a student to believe that their approval requires consistently extraordinary performances, intentionally or inadvertently. Conversely, some young perfectionists develop this trait in response to a total lack of parental expectations.[5]

Under the *social learning model,* children learn to imitate their parents' actual or perceived perfectionism. Some children with perfectionistic parents may learn to live by the unrealistic standards the parents set for themselves. Other children may merely perceive their parents to be ideal adults and will strive to achieve in order to be more like their "perfect" parents.[6]

Under the *social reaction model,* children become perfectionists in response to adversity such as physical, sexual, or psychological abuse or neglect. According to Flett and his fellow researchers, this child thinks, "If I am perfect, no one will hurt me."[7]

Under the *anxious rearing model,* a child becomes perfectionistic because her parents are overly concerned about making mistakes. These parents worry that they or their children may be imperfect or prone to making mistakes. As a result, the child may become excessively worried about making mistakes then develop the fear of failure that is a hallmark of perfectionism.[8]

Birth Order

Other researchers have suggested birth order may have a bearing on a person's propensity to become a perfectionist. Parents may feel insecure when faced with rearing their first child. In wanting to reward their children for every good deed, these parents may inadvertently encourage a child to develop a desire to achieve greater and greater goals, which may eventually lead to the child setting unrealistic goals for himself or herself.

Because firstborn children frequently spend their first few years without siblings, they find themselves largely in the company of adults. They often adhere to the social learning model described above: They learn to imitate adult speech patterns and behavior and, accordingly, expect themselves to achieve in the same manner adults do.[9] This doesn't mean, of course, that children born second, third, or last won't become perfectionists or that first-born children inevitably will be. But it shows another way people might adopt perfectionism as a strategy for life.

Media and Cultural Influences

The media—and especially US media—sends us very strong messages about what kind of people we should be. Movies, internet entertainment sites, television shows, magazines, and the advertisers who support them want us to believe that, if we consume the right products in just the right ways, we'll become perfect people. If we take an expensive study course, we'll get better test scores. If we join a fitness club, we'll obtain the body we see on TV. In short, we are led to believe that whatever our life looks and feels like right now is not enough, and that the means to fix that problem is available only through a product we can buy.

Americans are bombarded by the message that hard work brings rewards. We are led to believe that doing our best will earn us success—but no one stops to think of the costs of doing our best 100 percent of the time.[10] In recent years, economists have noted a marked increase in employee productivity, but it has brought few rewards.

Because of economic conditions, our real income declines despite our hard work. We spend less time with our loved ones because we work 60-hour weeks in one, two, or even three jobs. We may be putting forth our best efforts, but on the whole, we are less happy than we have ever been.

The Dangers of Perfectionism

The dangers of being a perfectionist may have become evident to you already. Some are obvious, but others are subtle and insidious.

Perfectionism affects your health. Perfectionism contributes to depression in both its mild and severe forms. It can raise your level of stress, which exacerbates to a range of illnesses and can lead to eating disorders.

Perfectionism also may affect your social experience. Self-oriented perfectionists often experience excessive worry about the way others perceive them, which can lead to social anxiety disorders. Other-oriented perfectionists may have difficulty controlling their criticism of others' behavior, which can adversely affect their relationships with family, friends, and coworkers.

Other perfectionists develop irrational beliefs and behaviors, such as extreme worrying and obsessive-compulsive disorder. Some sabotage themselves through procrastination in their work and creative lives; these people unconsciously believe that the longer they put off completing a task or producing something, the longer they avoid a potential failure.[11]

Not as frequently addressed in the perfectionist literature is the *spiritual danger* of perfectionism. By this I mean that perfectionism can prevent you from becoming the balanced, creative, and productive person you wish to be. I'll explore this issue in depth in the next chapter.

Addiction

People with perfectionism, or those who live with perfectionists, sometimes describe their behaviors in addictive terms. Plus, both serious addiction and perfectionism tend to breed all-or-nothing thinking.

Some theorists have posited that perfectionists on some level anticipate the disappointment that follows from setting high expectations. Once the perfectionist or someone else has failed to meet the perfectionist's expectations, the sense of disappointment rushes in, a sense that may be accompanied by a flood of brain chemicals that attempts to ameliorate the perfectionist's disappointment. This flood of neurochemicals may for some people, become addictive. In fact, it's the way many addictive drugs work, by stimulating certain parts of the brain to produce additional chemicals. The perfectionist may also feel relieved to be vindicated in expecting disappointment or may be hooked on experiencing disappointment.

It's not a stretch to believe addiction to drugs or alcohol might arise from being perfectionist if the person is uncomfortable with being a perfectionist. Drugs and alcohol might allow a perfectionist several minutes, or even hours, when he doesn't need to be in control of his own life. Drug and alcohol abuse, sex, or food might become a space of escape where perfectionists can let go for a little while. However, I haven't turned up any hard medical or psychological statistics demonstrating a link between perfectionism and addiction in my research. Still, based on my anecdotal observations, I believe there is a chance of addiction arising if those with perfectionist tendencies consistently fail to fill the gap between their potential and unrealistic standards, using chemical or compulsive behavior to escape the pain of the failure (see figure 1 on page 17).

Moving Beyond Perfectionism: A Healthy Goal

Seen in this light, moving beyond perfectionism is a healthy goal—and a realistic one. Because overcoming perfectionism is all about learning to set realistic and desirable goals.

By reading this book, you'll learn to identify the warning signs, dangerous behaviors, and irrational thoughts that accompany perfectionism, and then you'll learn how to overcome those practices. Some of these behaviors and thoughts can be corrected on your own, but for others, you may need to ask for the help of family, friends, your doctor, or mental health professionals. In the past, there was a stigma attached to going to therapy to get help. It meant you were crazy and unable to deal with your problems.

Today, however, seeking help is usually perceived as a sign of strength, of taking initiative and facing your problems head on. Please, as you read this book, if you see yourself headed into dangerous territory, seek the help you need and deserve. In an emergency, call 911. Researchers, therapists, and perfectionists alike have identified concrete benefits from overcoming perfectionism. Among these are the ability to try new things previously avoided because of the fear of failure or social stigma, becoming more confident and expressive, developing better relationships and new friendships, and decreasing your levels of depression and anxiety about making mistakes.[12]

CHAPTER 2

THE SPIRITUAL DANGER OF PERFECTIONISM

Perfection ... is a quest that causes us to doubt and denigrate ourselves, our true selves, our quirks and foibles and great leaps into the unknown, and that is bad enough.

—ANNA QUINDLEN[13]

We all carry phenomenal desires in our hearts—some spoken, some deeply hidden from even our closest friends. You may even have desires that you have forgotten about or let fall by the wayside: a desire to illustrate children's books, to act in a play, to learn to play the piano, to start a business, or to write a novel. In many cases, *perfectionism prevents you from attempting to do the thing that is the deepest longing of your heart because it carries the greatest risk if you fail.* This is another reason why perfectionism is spiritually dangerous: it can keep us from being the people we want to be.

By spirituality, I mean not only the mystical or religious experiences you may have, but also the whole range of energies that connect you with the world and other humans. I'm defining spirituality very broadly here because the word means something different for everyone, and I trust you'll apply your understanding of the concept to this chapter. For some, spirituality is a connection with wild spaces, while for others it may be contained entirely in religious practices. Others define spirituality as a centering, creative force.

The spiritual danger of perfectionism extends to all aspects of our lives: our work lives, creative lives, religious lives, family lives, and more. We adopt standards that the media or our parents or bosses say we need to achieve, but that are unrealistic for us, with our limited resources,[14] time, and energy. In the end, that means *we overlook our true potential* in the hopes of achieving someone else's unrealistic standards.

Say, for example, the work of Vincent Van Gogh inspires you to become a painter. You buy several lovely Van Gogh coffee table books, fill the walls of your home with Van Gogh prints—you even have a Van Gogh calendar at work. You also buy yourself an easel, some oil paints, a nice selection of brushes, and pre-stretched canvases from your local art store. As you lay down the color, you try to capture the master's strokes, his emotional energy. But you can't, so halfway through the project, you move the paints and the canvas to the closet. Eventually, you throw them away.

Does that sound familiar? It might not be painting for you. It might be a woodworking project you were inspired to undertake after watching *This Old House.* It might be a modest do-it-yourself renovation of your garage. It might be the novel, ten pages of which you wrote before realizing you're not John Irving or J. D. Salinger.

By trying to match wits with these extraordinarily gifted people, you've set an unrealistic standard for yourself. This doesn't mean you can't be a genius in your own right, but you're not going to be able to imitate precisely the style of any particular author or artist—nor should you because they've already done that work.

Acclaimed columnist and novelist Anna Quindlen insists that "Nothing important or meaningful, or beautiful, or interesting, or great ever came out of imitations. The thing that is really hard, and really amazing, is giving up on being perfect and beginning the work of becoming yourself."

Quindlen's insight pierces the heart of the matter. What perfectionism does is prevent you from developing your own style of writing, speaking, drawing, diving, or whatever else you want to do. As perfectionists, we set our sights so high that we set ourselves up for failure. We know failure is coming, and we fear it. So we put our projects aside before we finish them, or we don't even begin them. Before we get to about one-third of the way done, we allow ourselves to believe that whatever we're making is going to be perfect. It hasn't been fully formed yet, so our minds can't begin to criticize it. We might even believe our project is going to be the greatest thing ever.

We happily imagine the great success of our project. We will be the toast of the town, and awards will begin to line our shelves. As we get further along in the creation of our book, or art, or new business, the flaws begin to show. Our progress slows and then often stops without our ever *deciding* to abandon the project. Sometimes the stress of wanting to create something perfect paralyzes us altogether.

This pressure to achieve immediately at high levels begins at an early age.

A woman attending one of my workshops, whom I later coached on releasing her perfectionism, shared her story: "When I was a child in art class, we were given a blank canvas and paints. I really wanted to paint something beautiful, but every time the teacher came around, I was sitting in front of a blank canvas. I told her I was still thinking about it. In reality, I knew once I put a mark on the canvass there was no turning back—I couldn't erase it. This has been a metaphor for the way I've approached most everything in my life."

How can we move beyond this paralysis? We need to both be more *realistic* and more *imaginative* in our goals.

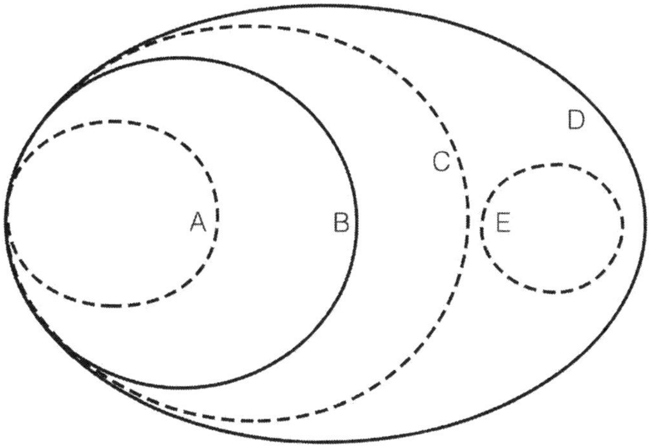

fig. 1

Let's look at figure 1. Each of the elliptical circles represents a different level of accomplishment or expectation. Circle *B* represents your current reality. This is the level of achievement you reach predictably and comfortably. Circle *C* represents your true potential. With some hard work and inspiration, you can expand your current reality into this larger circle.

Circle *D* represents a perfectionistic, unrealistic standard.

When you try to reach this level of accomplishment, the genius level of Van Gogh for example, two things may happen because you've set unrealistic goals. First, because you have failed to achieve these standards, you may find yourself retreating into the confines of circle *A*, which represents your minimum level of functioning.

You know you perform all of the activities within circle *A* very easily, and so you decide not to challenge yourself for a while. Second, you might spend some time flailing about in circle *E*, which represents the depression and addictive tendencies that often result from trying to cross an unbridgeable gap. If you persist in trying to reach the levels of accomplishment represented by circle *D*, eventually your unrealistic standards, your perfectionism, will produce low self-esteem, depression, anxiety, or shame. You'll stop taking risks altogether, and you'll find yourself back in circle *A*. These behaviors and beliefs keep you from developing fully as a confident, creative, productive, and spiritual individual.

Stop for a moment and think about how much the world would benefit if so many of us didn't stunt our growth as creative people, if we fully explored circle *C* instead of attempting a beeline for the outer edges of circle *D*. If we didn't hide our gifts because we feel they're not yet perfect, what would we gain?

Your Second Thing

Sometimes overcoming perfectionism means temporarily setting aside our biggest dreams if we can't seem to set goals other than unrealistic ones. If you want to be a singer, for example, but your definition of success is having a platinum album or starring in a Broadway musical, you may need to back-burner your dream until you can set more reasonable goals.

In the meantime, you can experiment with other things that fascinate you—activities and interests that are exciting but that you might not have fully explored yet. I know of others who have done this to great advantage.

When I used to write for entertainment industry publications, I found out something intriguing: Many people have been successful trying their "second thing," that is, pursuing their less risky, secondary goal.

For instance, Andrew Schneider and Diane Frolov became the head writers of *Northern Exposure,* one the most critically praised and highly rated shows of the 1990s. (And later, they were the writer-producers on the award-winning *The Sopranos.*) When they began in the entertainment industry, however, Diane had wanted to be a ballet dancer and Andrew an actor. It wasn't working out for either of them. Then some of their actor and writer friends suggested they try writing.

They began writing scripts and were successful almost immediately. Both Schneider and Frolov had been studying their respective crafts, dance and acting, for 10–15 years. Yet within a year or two of trying their hands at writing scripts, they were getting jobs to write television shows.

Corbin Bernsen, the actor best known for playing Arnold Becker on the TV show *L.A. Law*, dreamed of becoming a playwright. But he started going on acting auditions as a lark and got the jobs. People have been successful at their second thing or less risky, secondary goal, not only in the entertainment industry, but in business, art, and other areas.

Many people, even those who are not full-blown perfectionists, exhibit these tendencies when it comes to their dream job. They become extraordinarily idealistic and tense about the quality of the work they should be producing. It makes them afraid, and it makes them hesitate. They don't have the confidence they need for what they are doing. However, when they try another activity or job that sounds like it could be fun but is not their dream, they are not in emotional turmoil about it.

People trying their "second thing" don't possess the same fear. They're not concerned that if they are no good *at this*, they are no good *as people*. If their second thing doesn't work out, well, that's okay because it's not what they dreamed of anyway. (If we could wave a magic wand, we could decide that our first thing is our second thing and approach it like that. Unfortunately, that is not a valid approach because, in the back of your mind, you *do* know it is your number one thing.)

You can find value in trying out your second thing, even if you do not become successful with it.

Two tips for Second Thing success:

1. Pick something you can try right away—there should (usually) be no required classes before you try it. To get your hands on something, you can go to one of those ceramic stores where you buy an unfinished ceramic piece. The staff provides paints and paintbrushes, and you go for slathering on the paint and see what happens.

2. Write a bad poem, right now: Get out your phone and set the timer for six minutes. Write a rhyming poem of at least eight lines about something you remember from elementary school. Don't think, just press the timer, and go! (If you write a good poem in error, it's okay—I will give you a C+—but a bad poem is even better.)

Let yourself feel what it's like to be doing an activity for the sheer joy and adventure of it and not be bound up in the results.

I had a bit of success with stand-up comedy when I tried it as my less risky secondary goal. Because I'm a little rebel sometimes, I didn't follow my first tip above when it came to stand-up comedy. I *did* take a class. (There are open mic nights at comedy clubs all over the country, and you can go right up onstage and give it your best shot.)

I took a six-week course that focused on mining your life for funny stories. With a few stories in hand, we next wrote and edited them down, so we didn't waste too much time on the "set-up"—the first part of the joke the audience needs to hear to get the punchline. Finally we each stood in front of the class with a microphone and told our jokes.

Here is an example: "I was never good in math—basically, I *stopped* understanding math problems when they started putting *letters* in them."

Before getting it to the state above, I talked too much about what grade I was in when I started to struggle, mean math teachers—and none of that was needed for the joke. It was also important to put the punch "word"—the one that makes the joke come together, in this case "letters"—late in the final sentence.

The result? During the open mic performance at a comedy club following the class, I "killed," as comedians say. To see some of my comedy I used to do, go to https://www.youtube.com/watch?v=D2ahhEGYQZo

Social Dangers

Even when we set aside perfectionism in our creative and productive lives, we often refuse to set it aside in our relationships with other people. We may become frustrated when we can't express ourselves creatively and capture our brilliance in words, paint, websites, or whatever our chosen medium is. In our social lives, we're similarly scared to be ourselves, to display our full brilliance to friends and strangers, because we fear we'll be rejected. We're afraid we'll somehow reveal that we don't measure up or, worse, that we are frauds. Those of you who have joined a sports team or entered graduate school probably know this feeling: imposter syndrome kicks in. There's been some kind of mistake, and you accidentally made it on to the team or into the program. Suddenly, everyone else seems far more skilled or strong or bright than you are. And you vow to become as perfect as they seem to be.

In short, you try to imitate them. You forget your interests, deviate from your path, and lose part of yourself. Quindlen gently admonishes us to overcome this identity crisis by reaching back to a time when we were innocently whole, unmarked by the world. She asks us to think back on our early elementary school days when we were more interested in following our own lights than in pleasing those around us. We didn't care or didn't know, she writes, about taking on "the protective coloration of the expectations of those around [us]."[15]

Some of this social camouflage is imposed by the demands of your job or position in your community or society, but much of it is learned and internalized in less demanding situations. Writer Anne Lamott has a theory that our "psychic muscles" become cramped and paralyzed in an attempt to protect our spiritual wounds from further harm: our childhood torments, adolescent humiliations, or adult disappointments. By allowing our muscles to cramp in this fashion, she notes, we're limiting our full range of motion.

Perfectionism has a tendency to wound us in ways we never thought possible. It limits our achievements by fracturing us into fragments of our former selves. We're trying to be the perfect professional, the perfect parent to adorably brilliant children, the son or daughter who anticipates all the needs of an ailing parent, the generous and enlightened practitioner of our chosen faith, the exceptional athlete, the acclaimed artist. And none of us can be all of those things.

Lamott reminds us that it is a creative and physical perseverance, and not perfectionism—which she calls "a mean, frozen form of idealism"—that allows us to achieve our dreams. As you work through this book, think about relaxing the psychic muscles that have for so long been cramped. Think about stepping into the warmth of well-used creative muscles, of perseverance and creative play, and stepping out of the cold, stormy life of perfectionism.

CHAPTER 3

PERFECTIONISM, SOCIAL ANXIETY, OBSESSION, AND ADDICTION

Perfectionism, as opposed to pursuing excellence as a *high achiever* (see page 4), is predicated on a key irrational belief—that one must be perfect. So it's not too surprising that perfectionists are prone to experiencing other irrational beliefs as well. The perfection belief can lead to a wide range of behaviors that seem inexplicable to people who haven't experienced perfectionism or its related disorders.

Social Anxiety

Perfectionists may feel anxious around other people for a variety of reasons, but they are more likely than others to be self-critical because they spend so much time and energy evaluating themselves. Perfectionism researcher June Price Tangney calls the feelings associated with self-evaluation the "self-conscious emotions." These include shame, guilt, embarrassment, and pride. Socially prescribed and self-oriented perfectionists may be most prone to experiencing these emotions.

Self-oriented perfectionists are likely to feel some combination of these particular emotions if they fail to meet their own unrealistically high standards or, conversely, may feel pride when they do manage to meet these standards. Socially prescribed perfectionists may feel this same range of emotions when they are being evaluated, or *perceive* that others are evaluating them. Other-oriented perfectionists may feel shamed or embarrassed if someone they hold to high standards, such as a child, spouse, supervisor, or employee, fails to meet their high expectations in a public setting. This is because the other-oriented perfectionist thinks the behavior of others reflects poorly on *them*.

When perfectionists engage in self-criticism, they often underestimate themselves, especially in social situations where they feel they are being judged by both themselves and others. In *Perfectionism: Theory, Research, and Treatment*, Lynn Alden, Andrew Ryder, and Tanna Mellings note that while people with social anxiety are often recognized as being less socially skilled when compared to people without the same anxiety, "they rate themselves even more negatively than do objective observers. They also underestimate others' liking for them. Indeed, socially anxious people have been found to rate themselves negatively even when their behavior is indistinguishable from that of normal comparison groups." These researchers also note that certain groups of people, most notably musicians and actors, move in professional circles that require high standards of performance; these professionals are also more likely to have high standards for themselves, which can mean "debilitating anxiety when faced with an audience."[16]

Perfectionists with anxieties about social interaction or performance often try to avoid these situations, or they go to great extremes to make them bearable. Anxious perfectionists who must deliver a formal, public speech, for example, may spend hours preparing note cards on which they have written every word of their speech and then never lift their eyes from the words. These speakers end up betraying their anxieties and distancing themselves from their audiences. Other anxious perfectionists may have difficulty eating, drinking, singing, dancing, or playing sports when other people are watching, or they might struggle with going out if they aren't dressed immaculately. They may have difficulty engaging in casual conversations, dating, meeting new people, or asserting themselves.[17] In severe cases, social anxiety crosses over into social phobia, which provokes intense feelings of fear and panic in some of the most common social situations.[18]

For a perfectionist, overcoming social anxiety requires being aware of the negative statements she makes about herself or that she believes others are making about her. She must identify instances of self-criticism and construct positive counterstatements to her irrational beliefs. For more about positive counter-statements, see chapter 6.

CHAPTER 4

PERFECTIONISM AND PRODUCTIVITY

I talked a bit in chapter 2 about the spiritual dangers of perfectionism and how perfectionism can keep us from being our complete selves and from sharing our gifts with our friends, families, and communities. In this chapter and those that follow, I'll take a hard look at the perfectionist habits that limit the quantity and quality of our creative work. Even if you don't exhibit all these traits, you may want to read each section in this chapter because they contain good advice for all perfectionists.

Procrastination

Perhaps the most common problem among perfectionists is procrastination, and it's because we fear failure. If we never get around to finishing a project, or even to beginning it, then we are less likely to fail.[19] The project, because it remains perpetually unfinished, is neither a success nor a failure.

Because they tend to be conscientious and ambitious, self-oriented perfectionists are less likely to be procrastinators than are socially prescribed perfectionists. Being less intrinsically motivated, they live with "a sense of helplessness about the inability to establish personal control over evaluative standards and a sense of hopelessness about the inevitability of failure in the future."[20] In short, they're not sure how people will evaluate their work, and so they try to make their work be everything to everybody. This is impossible, and perfectionists know it. Accordingly, they rarely finish their work.

Despite the apparently simple steps that can be taken to remediate procrastination, the habit is difficult for perfectionists to overcome. In order to stop procrastinating, socially prescribed perfectionists must learn to accept less than perfect work from themselves and understand that others aren't expecting perfect work from them, either.

My recommendations for overcoming procrastination, therefore, focus on overcoming both perfectionism and procrastination.

Overcome Your Fear of Embarrassment

Many people, not only perfectionists, are paralyzed by the possibility of embarrassment at work, school, church, or in social situations. Learning to face our fears of embarrassment, especially if they involve social anxieties, helps us to be free. It's all right if you're not a dazzling conversationalist or a great dancer at parties—few people are! We benefit when we focus less on what people might think about us and more on opening up new opportunities for ourselves—even if it means risking a little embarrassment.

As an example, I'll share with you a story I heard about a man I'll call Steve. In his professional life, Steve was a high-achieving graphic artist and writer. Most of his work, however, was done alone, which was fine with him because he feared social embarrassment. When Steve became friends with another artist, she began inviting him to her parties, but he always declined the invitations. Helpfully, the friend persuaded Steve to be the very first person at the party; in fact, she asked him to help her set up for the party. That way, from the moment people started talking to one another, Steve would be present, and could, as he grew more comfortable, contribute to the conversations and meet new people. Within a few parties, Steve was coming out of his shell, so much so that, when he was offered a chance by a local newspaper to review local bands in clubs and bars,

Steve jumped at the chance. His columns became very popular with local musicians, many of whom befriended Steve. Today, Steve still feels a little social anxiety from time to time, but he has become less focused on what others might think of him, and more focused on trying to meet new people and collect new experiences and stories for his writing.

In my own life, this works, too. At a large business or social event, I tend to hang back. But at my church, where I am the minister, I feel like I am welcoming people—even those I have never met—to a place and a group I know well. So try Steve's idea: be one of the first people to an event, and be a resource to answer questions ("The bathroom is down the hall." Yes, there is a lovely balcony."), and it's like you are a co-host. Much more comfortable!

Trying to Be Just Average Occasionally

According to Allan Mallinger and Jeannette DeWyze, the authors of *Too Perfect: When Being in Control Gets Out of Control*, it's extremely important to "aim for average" periodically.[21] And no, you don't need to try to be average at those things that matter most to you. Aiming for average is a matter of accepting less than perfect performances in tasks that can become lower priorities. According to Mallinger and DeWyze, it's best to start small. They suggest catching up on writing emails by doing just that, writing emails without trying to be too witty or wise.

There are many ways to be average. Mallinger and DeWyze call it "being B-minus" in areas of your life that are not your biggest goals and biggest challenges.[22] If you go to the salon every month, you might let your hair grow out for an extra couple weeks (and maybe discover a new way to style it in the process). You might wear your shoes outside without polishing them first. Or maybe skip mowing the lawn this week. And so what if a photocopy print is a little crooked? The possibilities for average performances are endless!

And remember, while your performance may *feel* below average to you, you are simply striving to do the same amount of work that other people do. By letting up on yourself in the small things, you'll both free up time for the more important things in your life and perhaps gain more perspective on the bigger tasks as well.

Stop Worrying

We all worry. In fact, a little bit of worry might be healthy. It keeps us planning ahead (we'll be on time to the important meeting), it keeps us safe (we install smoke detectors), and it keeps us on our toes (we make sure our kids don't play in traffic). But it's important not to let worrying get out of hand. Mallinger and DeWyze point out that perfectionists tend to become preoccupied with worry and doubt, that is, they're so worried about so many things that they can't concentrate on any one task.[23]

Preoccupation and doubt contribute to perfectionists' procrastination because they think about all the possible outcomes of a project, including all the ways it might fail, and doubt that they can perform in accord with anyone else's expectations. *Overcoming worry is often a matter of learning to differentiate between rational thoughts and irrational ones.* In the working and creative world, these two kinds of thoughts are closely related to creativity and internal criticism. You'll learn more about the creative and critical voices in the next chapter.

Forget About Order

When I say forget about order, I don't mean that you should abandon yourself to chaos. In fact, being clear of physical and emotional clutter is key to productivity. But it's better that you don't hold yourself to specific patterns of behavior. If you're a writer, for example, you may feel you need to get *all* your research out of the way before you begin writing. You might think you need to draft some kind of outline so you know what to research, but you're not sure how best to organize it. In reality, you can do these tasks in any order. You don't necessarily *need* an outline to write, and you can begin writing without completing your research. You might create an outline based on what you find when you do your research, for example.

Overcoming procrastination, then, is learning to be flexible not just about results, but about the perceived order in which you must accomplish tasks.

Delegate

Sometimes we procrastinate because we feel overloaded with work, and we'll never be able to get it all done well. In this case, we need to learn to delegate, which is no easy task for many perfectionists.[24] We can't trust other people to undertake tasks that in the end will bear our names. However, we need to learn to trust that others have respect for us and will put in their best effort, efforts that we can polish before we pass them on to our supervisors, bosses, editors, publishers, or other authority figures.

If you're an academic, you can hire a research assistant to begin your work for you, and thus leapfrog your first instinct to procrastinate. If you have invited a dozen people over for a dinner party, you can bring in housekeepers to clean your house and have a neighborhood teenager mow your lawn. Taking the pressure off yourself is an important part of becoming a healthy person. It also frees up your time to focus on things that are more important to you, and that only you can do.

Start (or Finish) Something Right Now

That's right. It's time to put some of these principles into action. Put down this book before you read any further and start or finish one thing on which you've been procrastinating because of your perfectionist tendencies. Finish staining and varnishing that antique table or chest you bought five years ago. Catch up on correspondence with one friend, even if it means sending an email rather than composing a handwritten letter. Finishing filing last year's paperwork, even if you fear your filing system isn't yet ideal. Make progress on a long-abandoned project sitting in your closet, collecting dust in the garage, or hidden on your computer's hard drive. Once you get this one task out of the way, you may feel a great sense of relief, and perhaps even empowered to do others.

Other Self-Defeating Behaviors

Perfectionists participate in a broad range of behaviors that either contribute to actual failure or to the perception of failure. While not every perfectionist engages in all of the following behaviors, many perfectionists exhibit more than one of them.

Perfectionists can be moody.

One day we're thrilled with the high praise we've received on a project or performance, but the next day we're depressed because we believe we'll never achieve the same level again. Or we may become needlessly angry with ourselves or others for making it difficult to achieve perfection. The boss wants you to get the project done by next week—next week! How will you ever make the project perfect in that time frame? You can't, and you get angry at your boss for expecting too much from you, when in reality your boss probably understands that a week isn't going to be enough time to turn out stellar results. Chances are your boss hasn't had a chance to get the project done herself and has put it off until almost the last minute. Instead of thinking of such an assignment as an opportunity for failure, think of it as a vote of confidence in your ability to turn things around quickly and satisfactorily.

Perfectionists tally their achievements.

This tends to be a special problem among young perfectionists, who have ample opportunities to rack up 100 percent scores and A+ grades in school, and among perfectionists dedicated to a single sport or hobby. These perfectionists may count their trophies and ribbons without pausing to ask why these markers of distinction are important to them. In fact, aiming for a string of relatively easy achievements may keep us from tackling new physical, intellectual, and creative challenges.

If you've won the black-and-white photography division every year at your county fairs' arts competition, for example, why not enter the State Fair, get your work into a gallery, or even enter some of your color photos or paintings in the county competition? The variety and difficulty of your achievement and experiences can be more important than the sheer number of them in a single field.

Perfectionists tend not to live in the present.

This fact goes hand in hand with the previous two. It's fine to take time to enjoy your achievements, and there's nothing wrong with displaying a diploma or trophy on the wall and looking at them with a smile. Yet we may glory in our past successes instead of aiming for new ones in the present. We may fear the future because of past failures. We persuade ourselves that we'll do a better job on a project if we wait just a little longer to begin working on it. Rarely do we stop to think about what we're doing in this moment or the kind of creative or productive lives we're leading today. It's important to learn to live in the present. For perfectionists, the present can provide some breathing room between our successes and our perceived failures, both those in the past and in the future.

PERFECTIONISTS CAN LOSE PERSPECTIVE.

Miriam Adderholt and Jan Goldberg, in their book *Perfectionism: What's Bad About Being Too Good*, use the workings of a telescope to explain how perfectionists lack perspective on their work and lives. "When looking at the goals you haven't met," they write, "you use the magnifying end so they appear much larger than they really are. But when looking at those you have met, you use the 'minifying' end so they appear minute and insignificant."[25] In other words, we need to explore in which situations to apply certain critical tools, when to focus on details, and when the big picture is more important. Engaging in criticism out of proportion to the situation under consideration will only result in stress. When we explore—try different ways of thinking about how we respond—we can get free of doing the same thing over and over, and expecting different results.

Perfectionists tend to drill themselves until they get it right.

Perfectionists may exhibit behavior similar to that of people with obsessive-compulsive disorder (OCD). We may refuse to let something go until we get it *just right*, which in the end can do more harm than good. That may mean we rearrange flowers in bouquet until all we have left is tattered flowers and broken stems. Or we may practice our song for a community band or choral performance for hours until we have it down pat, only to learn that the director wants us to play it at a different tempo or in a different style. Perfectionists who engage in this behavior may indeed have some degree of OCD, or they may just want to make everything they do appear effortless.[26]

Perfectionists are famous for all-or-nothing thinking.[27]

We've all seen high school students with this habit; they agonize over the B+ on a report card that otherwise contains all A's. The advertising account executive may think herself a failure because she missed landing one big account, even though she's already improved her performance by 25 percent over the previous year. These perfectionists are prone to experiencing bouts of depression, anger, anxiety, or inadequacy.[28]

CHAPTER 5

OVERCOMING PARALYSIS:

THE POWER OF FAILURE

From what we've learned so far, then, it's not easy to be a perfectionist. We tend to be moody and overly critical of ourselves, to procrastinate and keep others at arm's length. Much of our frustration is directed at the work we leave unfinished and the goals we have not yet reached. So we become paralyzed; caught between the desire for success and the fear of failure, we don't know how to proceed. Learning to redefine our goals and to appreciate *all* the work we do—rather than just the stellar stuff—will help us become more creative, productive individuals.

The "Critical Voice" vs. the "Creative Voice"

As perfectionists, we often mistake our inner critics for our inner muses. We listen to our critical voices rather than our creative voices. For most of us, this is because our critical voice is very well developed; we've been using it for years to evaluate and criticize ourselves and perhaps even others. *Our creative voices are considerably less strong, in part because our critical voice is too busy shouting that we're going to fail at any creative pursuit we attempt.*

Julia Cameron, the author of *The Artist's Way*, identifies the sound bites coming from this critical voice as our "core negative beliefs." Among these negative beliefs are "I don't have good enough ideas," "I will do bad work, not know it, and look like a fool," and "It's too late, if I haven't become a [successful person] yet, I never will."[29]

Unfortunately, most of us have been repeating these core negative beliefs to ourselves for so long that we take them as truth, rather than as a bad habit. In Brené Brown's book *Daring Greatly*, she succinctly describes these core negative beliefs as some variation of "I am not enough."

Take a moment now and think of how you talk to yourself, the automatic monologue that runs in your head. These are the thoughts that, in big and small ways, bring you down and make you watch TV while eating a carton of ice cream, instead of creating something.

List here three of your core negative beliefs:

1. ______________________________

____

____

____

2. ______________________________

____

____

____

3. ______________________________

____

____

____

Julia Cameron has an interesting take on perfectionism. She says, "perfectionism is a refusal to let yourself move ahead. It is a loop—an obsessive, debilitating closed system that causes you to get stuck in the details ... and to lose sight of the whole."[30] This cycle, she proclaims, is not one of humility, or a quest to get everything just right, but rather an exercise in egotism. It's our own pride, she writes, that keeps us wanting to produce a perfect work.[31]

Getting out of this loop means learning to turn off our critical voices. Only when we silence our critical voices will we see clearly all the paths we can take away from our vicious circle of unrealistic expectations and anticipated failures. The best way to do this, according to many creative professionals, is to let yourself do bad work.

Bad work? You might think, *There's no way I'm going to turn in any projects or performances that are subpar.*

But here is the good news: You won't have to show this bad work to anyone. In fact, you can throw it in a drawer and not look at it for weeks—almost forget about it.

Anne Lamott calls the phenomenon "shitty first drafts." Lamott shares this secret about the best writers she knows: "Not *one* of them sits down routinely feeling wildly enthusiastic and confident. Not one of them writes elegant first drafts. All right, one of them does, but we do not like her very much."[32] So when you undertake your bad work—whatever it may be—know that the best in the business are couched in their homes, offices, and studios coughing up the same nasty stuff you are when you first sit down.

To become good at what you do, you need to be familiar with those in your field. English teachers will tell you that to write well, you need to read well.

An important book I read was John Irving's *The Cider House Rules.* Irving is both talented and prolific. I've learned a lot from reading this novel.

I came home from work one day, and I found *The Cider House Rules* open on the back of the sofa, which my then-wife was reading. Never a big novel reader, I started reading the book anyway. As I went through several pages, I was stunned at the quality of the writing. What he did with the sentences in his paragraphs and the beauty of it ... and how looking beneath the surface you could almost feel the iceberg of work and thinking he had done to have these paragraphs of insight and allure appear on the page. I was writing a stage play at the time, and this thought occurred to me: *There is no reason for me to write a single word of fiction while this guy is writing.*

I could easily tell how he was on a different planet from me as far as writing talent. And that was de-motivating for a while. Then I realized that we all have something to say, something to express. I have the ability I have in any given moment, and what I ought to do is just create.

You know, there is an old saying that "anything worth doing is worth doing *right.*"

Not true.

Zig Ziglar modified it in a helpful way: "Anything worth doing is worth doing *badly until* we learn to do it right."

I told my John Irving story to an audience at a speaking engagement, and at the end, a man stood up. He said, "You know, I have been a guitarist for 25 years, played in all kinds of bands, but I have never written a song. I have always wanted to write a song, but when I start writing … I know how bad it is."

Here is where the problem often lies: We have what you might call our "critical voice," or perhaps we can say your "evaluative voice." Right now, I am not using "critical voice" to mean self-criticism and self-condemnation. I mean it in the way we use our critical abilities to evaluate the quality of, say, a book. We study fiction in high school and possibly in college, and our teachers encourage us to be critics so we can tell what a good piece of writing is.

However, when we are fledgling creators, we are not able to produce a good piece of writing right away. A gap exists, and our paralysis (again) comes from trying to bridge that gap. The gap is from our ability to critically evaluate our work being at a nine out of ten, and our ability to create good work is a one out of ten. Your evaluative abilities get a lot more practice in your life than your creative abilities do.

And so the guitarist mentioned above said, "I have never written a song because I start, and I know that it sucks." And then he said, happily, "What you just explained about the critical voice and the creative voice actually opened things up for me. What I am going to go do right now is go home and write a shitty song!"

The audience cheered for him! And that was a beautiful moment. He was free.

We take a big step toward freedom when, in our creative lives, we say, "Yeah, let me just write what I can, and the song is going to be however good it is. I am going to try to make it good, but until I get some experience, it's probably going to be fairly crummy."

But that's okay, because we mine the crummy stuff until we uncover the gold.

Sometimes, when you're writing or creating something you value, you need to keep this mantra in your head, "Crappy song, crappy song, crappy song"—or substitute Anne Lamott's phrase "shitty first draft." Sometimes that will help, and if you manage to get all the bad work out, you'll begin to hit your stride and really create something you like. But sometimes you'll need to go beyond that, to let yourself work on a project so infinitesimally small that you can't even think of it as needing drafts. I know I'm not alone in feeling this way, because many artists and other creative people have expressed how difficult it is to face the blank page or canvas, to even get a rough sketch down.

My solution? Shrink the canvas. Build one-half of a quilt block. Write on a sticky note or index card. See how many melodies you can sing within a single scale. Anne Lamott counsels her writing students to tackle small assignments because they're less daunting. Small assignments don't give our critical voices time to develop into a clamor.[33] You can dedicate yourself to one small thing for a set amount of time. Instead of sitting down to write your novel, for example, you can dedicate 20 or 30 minutes to drafting a short-short, which is a story that's less than two pages long—a mere fraction of one scene. Once you've written one short-short, you can file it away and on another day write another one. Because there's no pressure to go anywhere with these efforts, or to show them to anyone, you're able to be productive, even if in fits and starts, time after time.

You shouldn't even *think* that the results might become part of a scene, which might become part of a chapter, which might become part of a novel. The idea is to get a big, fat pile of papers in a file folder, just to show yourself that you can be productive.

After some time, you can let yourself tackle larger projects, but keep the same principle in mind: You're aiming to be productive, not fantastic. Keep your critical voice turned off. After several weeks of practicing these short exercises, you'll find that your writing, art, or whatever else you're working on actually has become better. You use the passive voice less frequently than you used to in your writing, your brush strokes are less tentative, your tenor range has grown stronger.

In short, you've accomplished something worthwhile, achieved something beautiful—however small—without expecting yourself to accomplish anything at all. I know of a poet who, when she's not feeling good about her writing, will compose only sonnets. "How much," she asks herself, "could I mess up in 140 syllables? And so few people read sonnets anyway." Still, after a month, she has 30 poems.

Recently I also heard a story of creative writing advice given by the great science fiction writer, Ray Bradbury. He suggested, instead of starting out with a novel, that newbies write one short story per week for a year. "Because," Bradbury points out, "it is impossible to write 52 bad short stories." Guaranteed success!

The Power of Failure

Eventually, we all want recognition for our talents, some acknowledgement of our creative work. We work up the courage to show our efforts to somebody. But the people in our writing workshop scrawl all over our short story, the local coffee shop turns down our paintings, our boss tells us our ideas are underdeveloped and unsupportable. We feel like a failure. We begin again our cycle of negative, perfectionistic thinking: *I'll never be a great artist. I'll never get a promotion. I've invested all this money in these silly riding clothes—all for nothing.*

At this point, it's time to gain some perspective. We're talking about one judge who had the sun in her eyes, one cafe owner who might not know good taste if he tripped over it, one small group of novice writers who, you know from reading *their* stuff, aren't particularly talented themselves. (Of course, we shouldn't get into a game where we belittle everyone's negative opinions—because some of them may be valid—but we do need to understand this rejection may only be temporary.) Also, remember that getting turned down could be the result of some factor having nothing to do with you. For example, it may be that the spot in the coffee shop was already promised to another artist.

I know of a university professor who teaches a lot of very bright first-year students. They come to her class in the fall, they write their first papers, and many of them get low B's or C's. They accuse her of grading too harshly, and she explains that she has not been unduly cruel in her comments. Then a few freshmen will start to cry. They talk about the pressure put on them by their parents, or how they've always earned straight A's, and now their winning streaks are over, and they're going to flunk out of college.

The professor passes them some tissues, sits back in her chair, and listens for a while, nodding sympathetically. Then she tells them that she—with her PhD framed on the wall, the photos of happy children on the desk, and her published books on the shelf behind her—was once a straight-A student herself. This fact doesn't surprise them. Straight-A students tend to have a good deal of respect for high achievers. However, what she tells them next does surprise them.

> "You know what was the greatest thing that ever happened to me as a student?"
>
> The freshman typically shakes her head, trying to stem her tears.
>
> "I failed a class."
>
> The student before her opens her eyes wide and maybe cracks a tiny smile.
>
> "In 10th grade, I brought home one report card with straight A's and an F. The F was in math, and it was for a class I had repeated—a class in which I had earned a C the first time. I did *worse* the second time through. And you know what happened?"
>
> "Your parents must have been mad."

> "No, Mom and Dad were teachers, so they knew that grades really meant very little most of the time. Instead, they said, "Well, maybe it's time to move on to something else."
>
> "I tried twice, failed, and learned that maybe trigonometry wasn't for me. So I dropped out of math since I had already completed the requirements for college. I transferred into a creative writing class instead, and I found I loved writing, and years later, I even earned a Master's degree in it."
>
> "You still got into all your colleges?"
>
> "Well, no ... My back-up school turned me down, but the others didn't bat an eyelash. My point is that this one C isn't going to kill you. You can still get an A in the class, if that's what you want. It's not going to be a matter of working harder, just working better. Let's work together, in fact, to be sure you understand the next assignment."

And suddenly, having found an ally where she thought she had an enemy, the freshman shakes the professor's hand and walks out of the office willing to try again. Her life isn't over. *Her parents* may be miffed, but hey, she's in college, she's an adult, she doesn't need to reveal her little failure to anyone.

Neither do you. So you fail at one thing—maybe even at something that really matters to you right now. That doesn't mean you're going to fail at it every time, and it certainly doesn't mean you're going to fail at everything.

In fact, what you and the freshman see as failure isn't really failure. It's just C-level work. It is, in other words, average. And it's OK to be average every once in a while.

CHAPTER 6

FROM PERFECTIONIST TO HIGH ACHIEVER:

OVERCOMING PERFECTIONISM TO INCREASE PRODUCTIVITY

While advice on dealing with perfectionism has been sprinkled throughout this book, this chapter both consolidates that advice and introduces tried-and-true remedies for perfectionistic behaviors. Not all of these tips, activities, and exercises will work for everyone, but now that you have a better understanding of perfectionism, you should be able to find a combination of remedies that applies to your particular situation.

I've broken this chapter into two primary sections: small changes and big changes. You can read them in whatever order you like, but I discuss smaller changes first because they're less daunting. If you begin to make the smaller changes, the bigger changes may follow more easily. Or the other way around may work for you. Maybe you're a details person, maybe you're a big-picture person.

Smaller Changes

1. Redefine Success

Whoa, you say. That's an awfully big change to include in this section, isn't it? Well, yes. It's a major change in your mindset, but it begins with small, simple steps. For a perfectionist, the only way to be successful is to be perfect. But since we know that we'll never be perfect in everyone's eyes in any given aspect of our lives, we might as well shelve our goal of perfection.

Let's replace the pursuit of perfection with the pursuit of excellence. If you seek excellence, you're seeking to advance, to move forward, to perform better. To perform better than whom? Yourself. To surpass your previous work. You should be in competition with no one but yourself—

the self that has accomplished some productive and creative work, but who wants to improve upon that work.

By pursuing excellence instead of perfection, we're allowing ourselves to move forward, rather than being paralyzed by a sense of despair or the anticipation of failure. Achieving excellence can't be done all in one fell swoop—believing that it can is perfectionistic thinking. Instead, we need to think of excellence not as a final goal, but as a process. In other words, in whatever aspects of your life you most value, you should aim to take yourself one or two steps beyond where you are now.

We have, then, redefined success as taking one or two steps. This new definition allows us multiple successes, rather than one big, hoped-for, success. We're setting reasonable standards and goals. We become high achievers instead of perfectionists.

A simple but effective strategy for us to change our thinking, such as setting reasonable goals, is the use of affirmations. I know, some people, maybe including you, think affirmations are stupid, or too new-agey. But their purpose is to counter the avalanche of habitual negative thinking that plays in our brains. Really, these automatic negative thoughts *are* affirmations. Since you are doing affirmations anyway, let's make them helpful to you. Let's do them on purpose.

2. Use Positive Counterstatements to Silence Your Inner Critics

Many therapists agree that one of the most useful exercises for people who suffer from a broad range of harmful personality traits and disorders—including depression, perfectionism, OCD, and anxiety—is to identify negative or otherwise harmful thoughts and behaviors and replace them with positive ones.

Learning this skill is key to overcoming perfectionism. When you're working on a project, your inner critic nibbles at your self-confidence and sets unrealistic standards. Let's say you're writing a paper for school. Your inner critic might say, "I need an A on this paper. If I don't get an A, it means the professor doesn't like me, and it's important that this professor likes me because I want to do research with him. I need to stay up all night and do as many drafts as it takes to get this paper perfect."

While sitting here analyzing this perfectionist's inner criticism from a distance, it's pretty easy for us to point out that there's very little correlation between earning a high score on something and being a likable or employable person. But it's hard for the paper writer to think as objectively as we can. If she's already put several days' work into a four- to five-page paper, for example, it may be time to stop working and be satisfied with what she has. What are some positive counter-statements she could use to gain perspective on her situation? Let's try these:

> "I am smart and can do this. I really want an A, but I've heard Professor Garcia's a hard grader. Maybe getting a B from him is the same as getting an A in another course."
>
> "I am not limited to my faulty assumptions. I have already achieved targets I have set for myself. I have the ability to do well, including on this paper."
>
> "I will call a friend who knows how my perfectionism can make me lose perspective and check in with her. She's good at helping me see clearly and set realistic goals."

If you're a perfectionist, chances are you've found yourself in a similar situation to this student's. You may have thought, for example, *this painting needs to be the first in a fantastic series that will get me my first gallery opening; my promotion hinges on this project; if little Timmy doesn't make it into the gifted program, it means I'm a failure as a parent;* or *if I don't get this job, my life is over.*

Again, this all-or-nothing thinking needs to be remediated with positive counter-statements. Stop and think positively. Short positive affirmations can help. Things like the following:

All is well, I'm okay, or *everything is alright.*

Charles Fillmore, cofounder of the Unity denomination, came up with this affirmation in his 90s, and I have found it useful to get myself started:

> "I fairly sizzle with zeal and enthusiasm and spring forth with a mighty faith to do the things that ought to be done by me."

Reframing affirmations to fit your specific circumstances can be useful:

> "Let's take this one painting at a time. Maybe the painting will be better if I let myself play with the art. Art doesn't have to be about pain and suffering!"
>
> "My boss trusts me. My entire pattern of work will contribute to my promotion, not just one thing."

And sometimes, when under the stress of your perfectionistic thinking, a spiritual choice can be simply saying, "God, help me." I have found that simple affirmation, or prayer, to transform the moment for me. It gets my mind and heart open for solutions I'm too stressed to see. Generally, I feel helped right away with a change in perspective and a reduction in worry.

3. Turn Problems into Opportunities

This is variation on the old sayings "Every cloud has a silver lining" and "When life gives you lemons, make lemonade." Some of the positive counterstatements in the previous paragraphs provide ways to turn problems into opportunities.

The school doesn't recognize your son's type of giftedness? Find people who do, and who can help him develop his talents.

You're not happy with the direction your project's taking at work? Ask your boss if you might look at it from a fresh perspective—one that excites you and that perhaps the company hasn't yet considered.

Does your painted self-portrait look more like an alien than it does you? Then let it become an alien—after all, X-rays of some of the world's most famous paintings show artists took their work in dramatically different directions than they had originally intended.

Nobody's responding to your resumes? Do some research to find out in what complementary fields you might use your skills or apply for positions in different departments of the same organization. Maybe a science museum won't hire you to deliver its classroom outreach presentations because your degree is in psychology or statistics instead of education or science, but that doesn't mean you can't apply for the open position evaluating those same programs.

What are some positive counter-statements to the negative statements you listed in chapter 5? Remember to make them simple and make declarations:

I am full of energy to get this done. All my knowledge and wisdom is available to me now. Walking a mile clears my mind and blesses my body.

Now you try it below:

1. ______________________________

____

____

____

____

2. ______________________________

____

____

____

____

3. ______________________________

____

____

____

____

4. Deal with Procrastination

As we saw in chapter 5, perfectionism and procrastination often go hand in hand. Overcoming procrastination takes practice and a bit of finesse. This may mean allowing extra time to complete a project, breaking a project down into smaller pieces, or removing distractions from our workplace. These tricks may help a lot of people.

Some of us, however, develop elaborate means of procrastination. For example, I might have intended to write half a chapter of this book each night over the course of two weeks. I might think that breaking the work into smaller steps will help me accomplish it. Instead, I might find myself writing three chapters the night before the workshop where I want to introduce it. And that's not going to produce high-quality work.

So instead, I *set up deadlines where I have to show my work to people.* Maybe I join a reading group for people working on similar projects. And every week, we swap chapters and get feedback. I don't want to embarrass myself by not showing up week after week with empty hands, while my fellow writers are plowing through their work—and getting great feedback from their peers at the same time. So if I turn in my work on time, I get twice the reward: the satisfaction of knowing that a chunk of it is finished—no matter how imperfect it may be at this moment—and also the feedback of a talented bunch of writers who work in my field. This trick has worked for many writers. I'm certain you can find a way to adapt it to your situation, no matter what your field.

5. Get Up and Get Out

Sometimes we need to take our minds off our work and ourselves. Taking a walk, going to see a movie, enjoying dinner or lunch at a cafe, or doing some serious exercise can help to clear your mind. Exercise also gets your blood flowing, which means you'll be refreshed and ready to tackle your project with new eyes when you return.

6. Use the Buddy System

Other people can help us gain perspective on our perfectionism. You may find this support in a trusted friend, a spouse, a therapist, a minister, or even someone else who's making a serious effort to stop being so perfectionistic. When you get stuck, you can meet with your buddy, or call him up, and get his take on the situation. Or I'm available if you want coaching: www.JohnConnor.com-

7. Reward Yourself

This is so important! Perfectionists crave positive feedback from others. It's why we work so hard at making everything just so. We need to provide that feedback for ourselves. If you're a self-oriented perfectionist, rewarding yourself may be as simple as taking a night off from working on you project to allow yourself a little perspective and some time when you're not obsessing. Or it might take the form of a chocolate bar.

Big Changes

1. Avoid Burnout

This may seem like a small thing, but it's huge. Why?

- You need to keep your energy up so that you can keep working at what matters to you.
- Burnout isn't healthy physically, spiritually, emotionally, or psychologically.
- Burnout keeps us from wanting to tackle new challenges or from addressing old ones.

How do you avoid burnout? You give yourself breaks—physical breaks, yes, but also those spiritual breaks that we perfectionists rarely allow ourselves. We need entire days, even weeks, when we allow ourselves to be wholly imperfect, to let the housekeeping or our correspondence slide a bit.

For some people, avoiding burnout means getting out of the house and socializing. For others, it means a day or a week of solitude at home, in your favorite location for reflection, or in an entirely new place you've never visited. Experiment with a combination of these to see what works for you.

2. Plan Positive Alternative Paths

I said earlier that you need to turn problems into opportunities - to make lemonade from lemons. But sometimes it's best if you don't let yourself end up with lemons in the first place.

This is where perspective comes in. Try to look past today, past your current project or relationship, or whatever you're focused on right now. Examine your present to see if you're headed in a positive direction—and more importantly, a direction where you want to be headed. If you feel you're going nowhere, or nowhere you'd like to end up, it's time to explore some new paths.

Sometimes we can explore these new paths right away—we can take guitar lessons if we've never played guitar, or -- if the timing's right -- we can move to a new town. But in most cases, we have to plan for these new paths. I like to think of this planning as building forks in the road before you even arrive at them.

Say you're a librarian at a public library right now, and you're getting tired of being a librarian. You enjoy keeping things in order, and you really like sharing your knowledge with people. You have some ideas about what kind of careers you might like to pursue in the future that would allow you to use those skills you like to use. Maybe you're interested in museum conservation or historic preservation. Maybe you're interested in becoming an elementary school teacher. You can't just wait for these forks in the road to show up because they won't just appear magically before you.

Instead, you plan for them. You attend lectures given at your local museums to learn more about their collections then volunteer at one of their events. You take some classes in early childhood education to get a head start on your teaching credentials. Then, when a job opens up, or when your spouse suddenly has to transfer to a job in another town, you're prepared to start a new phase in your life.

This advice doesn't only apply to your work life. You can prepare yourself to engage in spiritual quest, to enter into a long-term relationship, to make a major life change like retirement, or whatever other positive paths you imagine you might want to follow.

Which leads us to our next big change ...

3. Rebalance Your Life

Assess what's important to you. Are the activities in which you're striving to be perfect really the things that matter to you? Is keeping an immaculate house what defines you? Does the job you work at 50 hours a week show who you are?

Have you been hankering for a spiritual life or to reconnect with old friends or extended family members? Take a few moments each day to ask yourself if what you're doing *really* matters to you. And if it doesn't, stop doing it, or don't allow it to take up more of your time and mental energy. Or plan your transition away from it.

Final Thoughts

Remember that being less than perfect means being fully human; people love their friends and families for their personalities, thoughtfulness, even their quirks—not for their achievements. (In fact, some people have difficulty relating to extremely high-achieving people.)

Look around you. Have you become so obsessed with being perfect in one aspect of your life that you've neglected other aspects?

Always remember: Change is possible, especially for imperfect beings like ourselves. With a bit of reflection and effort, we can move toward ever greater achievements. *We can be creative, productive people, which is far better, and far more interesting, than being perfect people.*

Remember, too, that overcoming perfectionism takes a spiritual effort as much as it does material, emotional, and psychological ones. It's a process of reassembling these fragments of ourselves so that they make sense, a one-of-a-kind mosaic of our material realities, talents, hopes, and dreams. It's a matter of using these pieces to begin to fill in circle *C* from figure 1, laying piece by shattered piece, until you have a beautiful crazy design of a life. This is a process that requires serious reflection, some hard work, and—most importantly—a willingness to play and create.

One helpful example of a success story is with a woman I coached named Susan. She attended a talk I gave on overcoming perfectionism, and wanted to work on an upcoming challenge.

She is a lawyer, and was developing her law practice. She joined a "leads club"—a group of about 20 small business owners and marketers who meet weekly for breakfast to help each other promote their businesses. At each meeting members give a 30-second explanation of their business and what kind of leads they are looking for. Then one member will give a 20-minute talk that gives useful tips and also highlights the member's knowledge.

Susan was asked to give a talk on estate planning, to show members how to pass down their assets or businesses to their children. Simple, right?

When Susan called me, though, she was stressed by what to talk about, and the preparation.

> "What have you done so far?"
>
> "Well," she said, "I want to be thorough. So I have gone back to the Egyptians, to research the earliest records of people handing down belongings—"
>
> "Wait. Okay, Susan, I get it. I get wanting to be thorough—as perfectionists we sometimes worry we are being lazy. So we counteract that with detail."
>
> "But shouldn't I give them the history of how estate planning developed?"

> "No."
>
> "No?"
>
> "No," I said. "No one in the room cares about the history of estate planning. They want to hear in simple, non-lawyer terms, how their kids can inherit their money while paying the least amount in taxes on it."
>
> "That's easy. I can do that off the top of my head," Susan said.

And she did. And her audience loved getting the information.

In our coaching sessions, it became clear that other areas of her life were blocked by her perfectionism. For instance, although she wanted to have children, and her husband did too, she wasn't ready.

When I asked her what aspects of her life and circumstances she needed to change to be ready, she couldn't really answer. Money was no problem, they owned a house with plenty of space, her relationship with her husband felt good and stable.

> "I think you are waiting for a guarantee," I said.
>
> "Of what?"
>
> "As a potential parent, what do you want?"
>
> "I want to make sure I don't screw up my child. I want to be a good Mom. I'm waiting until I'm sure I'll be a good Mom."

"And when will that certainty come, that you'll be a good Mom?"

"Oh my God ..."

Susan realized she wanted a guarantee in advance that she would be the good mother of a happy, healthy, successful child. And while that is a good goal, if she waited for that guarantee to arrive in a certificate in the mail, she would wait forever.

After a few sessions, she felt good about her progress and worked on things on her own.

Less than a year later, she wrote me a letter describing how much she was helped: She was stepping forward more in her career and advancing, she was actively enjoying the talks in her leads group, and she was happily pregnant with her first child!

Two years later we talked again, and she was by then a judge!

When you take a step and begin to identify your perfectionistic thoughts and "pull the plug" on the habitual negative recordings that play in your head, opportunities literally open up for you.

A saying credited to the philosopher and writer Goethe goes, "Be bold, and mighty forces will come to your aid."

Sometimes my affirmation will be, "Go risk making a mistake!"

Or maybe just simply affirm: BE BOLD!

In whatever avenue of expression is important to you, go write a crummy song! The beauty that is *waiting* to come out of you is percolating just below the surface...

AN INVITATION TO CONNECT

If you would enjoy an occasional newsletter, and an online community of folks releasing perfect and making progress, subscribe here at **www.JohnConnor.com**.

There will be tips and stories and interviews on letting out the gold within you. It will also let you know about workshops that I periodically present.

ACKNOWLEDGEMENTS

The first person outside of my family that was very important to me was Dr. Walter Bahan, the minister of my church growing up.

Walter, you demonstrated strength and heart, and a spiritual dedication and joy that inspired everyone in my family. People you influenced in the 1960's and 70's at a spiritual community in Epping NH are *still* blessed by you, 40 years after you moved into the next life. Thank you.

Being free (or at least free-er) of the perfectionistic straitjacket helps you create. Two men who helped foster my creativity were my high school drama teacher, George Keith, and my high school Speech teacher, Larry Ross.

George, you welcomed all the mis-fit toys into your classroom, and you saw us. *Saw* us, beyond the neediness and nerdy-ness while we tried to be cool. We, like many high school theatre students, became a tribe. And finding your tribe, with a good "chief", is a very good thing.

Larry, you are beloved by the hundreds of debaters and performers you took to Speech tournaments over the years. And also by the regular students you taught who, terrified, had to do their first speeches in your class. You should be on the poster that they use in education programs that says, "You will make a difference in young people's lives."

ABOUT THE AUTHOR

JOHN CONNOR has first-hand experience with the challenges of perfectionism, and the freedom that results from confronting the faulty unconscious beliefs that cause the drive to be perfect.

John has tried and succeeded, and tried and failed. He failed at getting a sketch-comedy TV show on the air. But succeeded at making the pilot episode, getting network meetings to pitch more shows, and winning an award at a film festival. He failed the first time he tried stand-up comedy. But succeeded in becoming a touring comic, doing 70 shows in one year before retiring.

He dropped out of his first couple of college classes, but finally succeeded in getting his bachelor's degree — at age 46. And at age 55 he achieved a goal he had in the back of his mind and heart since adolescence — he leads a Unity congregation in Austin, Texas: Unity of Lake Travis.

John lives in Austin, and has two grown daughters whom he loves. He is a somewhat surprisingly poor drummer, considering that he first took lessons in third grade. "But I like drumming, so it doesn't matter how good I am," he just insisted in my head, since John is writing this all third-person and professional-like. He also is going to shamelessly tell you that he used to teach disco dance lessons in 1979; he forgot a prop in his first play; he will always treasure a college professor saying of a piece of his writing, "I could see that in 'The New Yorker'"; he is honored to work as a spiritual care counselor in hospice.

Some of his favorite moments have been seeing the light go on for someone in his workshops, when they "get" how their perfectionist thoughts have kept them trapped. Sometimes they begin laughing, because they see the prison they've been in, and their recognition begins to open the jail door…

ENDNOTES

CHAPTER 1

1. Gordon L. Flett and Paul L. Hewitt, "Perfectionism and Maladjustment: An Overview of Theoretical, Definitional, and Treatment Issues." In *Perfectionism: Theory, Research, and Treatment.* Ed. Gordon L. Flett and Paul L. Hewitt. Washington D.C.: American Psychological Association, 2002. p. 5.

2. Allan Mallinger and Jeanette DeWyze, *Too Perfect: When Being in Control Gets Out of Control.* New York: Clarkson Potter, 1992. p. 38.

3. William J. Knaus, *Do It Now! Break the Procrastination Habit.* New York: John Wiley & Sons, Inc, 1998. p. 103.

4. Flett and Hewitt, 14.

5. Flett and Hewitt, 90-91.

6. Flett and Hewitt, 91.

7. Flett and Hewitt, 93-94.

8. Flett and Hewitt, 95.

9. Adderholt and Goldberg, 9.

10. Robert B. Slaney, Kenneth G. Rice, and Jeffrey S. Ashby, "A Programmatic Approach to Measuring Perfectionism: The Almost Perfect Scales." In *Perfectionism: Theory, Research, and Treatment.* Ed. Gordon L. Flett and Paul L. Hewitt. Washington, D.C.: American Psychological Association, 2002. p. 82.

11. Robert B. Slaney, Kenneth G. Rice, and Jeffrey S. Ashby, "A Programmatic Approach to Measuring Perfectionism: The Almost Perfect Scales," in *Perfectionism: Theory, Research, and Treatment.* ed. Gordon L. Flett and Paul L. Hewitt (Washington, DC: American Psychological Association, 2002), 82.

12. Flett and Hewitt, 24.

Chapter 2

13. Quindlen, Mount Holyoke commencement speech. Mount Holyoke College, May 23, 1999. http://www.mtholyoke.edu/offices/comm/oped/Quindlen.shtml. Accessed 12 Dec. 2003.

14. Anna Quindlen, "Mount Holyoke commencement speech," Mount Holyoke College, May 23, 1999, Accessed 12 Dec. 2003. http://www.mtholyoke.edu/offices/comm/oped/Quindlen.shtml.

15. Quindlen, Mount Holyoke commencement speech.

CHAPTER 3

16. Alden, Ryder, and Mellings, 387.

17. Antony Swinson, 190.

18. Antony and Swinson, 192.

19. Gordon L. Flett, Paul L. Hewitt, and Thomas R. Martin, "Dimensions of Perfectionism and Procrastination." In *Procrastination and Task Avoidance: Theory, Research, and Treatment.* Ed. Joseph F. Ferrarri, judith L. Johnson, and William G. McCown, et. al. New York: Plenum Press, 1995. p. 114.

CHAPTER 4

20. Flett, Hewitt, and Martin, 119.

21. Mallinger and DeWyze, 58-59.

22. Mallinger and DeWyze, 58-59.

23. Mallinger and DyWyze, 135.

24. Flett, Hewitt, and Martin, 115.

25. Adderholt and Goldberg, 20.

26. Adderholt and Goldberg, 21.

27. Adderholt and Goldberg, 21, Antony and Swinson, 51

28. Antony and Swinson, 52

Chapter 5

29. Julia Cameron, *The Artist's Way: A Spiritual Path to Higher Creativity,* (New York: Jeremy P. Tarcher/ Putnam, 2002), 30-31.

30. Cameron, 119.

31. Cameron, 120.

32. Anne Lamott, *Bird by Bird: Some Instructions on Writing and Life* (New York: Anchor, 1995), 22.

33. Lamott,16.